Powerful Presentation Skills

A quick and handy guide for any manager or business owner

CAREER PRESS
180 Fifth Avenue
P.O. Box 34
Hawthorne, NJ 07507
1-800-CAREER-1
201-427-0229 (outside U.S.)
FAX: 201-427-2037

POWERFUL PRESENTATION SKILLS
A QUICK AND HANDY GUIDE FOR ANY MANAGER OR BUSINESS OWNER
ISBN 1-56414-109-8, $8.95
Cover design by Digital Perspectives
Printed in the U.S.A. by Book-mart Press

To order this title by mail, please include price as noted above,
$2.50 handling per order, and $1.00 for each book ordered. Send
to: Career Press, Inc., 180 Fifth Ave., P.O. Box 34, Hawthorne,
NJ 07507

Or call toll-free 1-800-CAREER-1 (Canada: 201-427-0229) to
order using VISA or MasterCard, or for further information on
books from Career Press.

Library of Congress Cataloging-in-Publication Data

Powerful presentation skills : a quick and handy guide for any
    manager or business owner.
        p. cm. -- (Business desk reference)
    ISBN 1-56414-109-8 : $8.95
    1. Business presentations. I. Career Press Inc. II. Series.
HF5718.22.P69   1993
658. 4'52--dc20   93-22387
                                                              CIP

TABLE OF CONTENTS

INTRODUCTION

While listening to an unusually inspiring speaker or dynamic presenter, have you ever had thoughts such as:

- I wish I could speak like that.

- If I could speak better I know I would be promoted.

- If only I could make better presentations I know my sales would increase.

- I am sure my inability to make effective presentations is holding me back at work.

If so, you're not alone. Most people *wish* they could be better public speakers and presenters. Few, however, do anything about it. By reading this book you are taking the first step toward making yourself a more dynamic presenter and a more inspiring public speaker.

For a business owner or executive, good presentation skills are a must. Whether you're making a presentation to the board of directors, explaining the marketing plan to your staff or simply presenting your budget to the boss, it's important for you to be able to do so in a professional, convincing manner.

Powerful Presentation Skills has been designed to help you learn how to be a better public speaker and presenter. You will learn everything you need to know from how to adequately prepare for your presentation to what to do after the presentation's over. Additionally, you will learn how to overcome what most people consider to be the biggest hurdle in public speaking — fear.

You owe it to yourself and your employer to improve your public speaking and presentation skills. If you do, it is inevitable that you will do better at work.

But there's more! If you're asking yourself, "But what's in it for me?" the answer is "plenty!"

John Ruskin said, "The highest reward for toil is not what you get from it, but what you become by it." If this is true, then your reward for becoming a more dynamic speaker will not have as much to do with what you get as it will with what you become.

Your life will be enhanced while you strive to improve your ability to make presentations. You will find that some important attitudes and habits will change — for the better. They will not lie dormant until the day when you "arrive" at being a good presenter. They will improve as soon as — and as long as — you move forward toward your speaking goal. It can change your life!

Let's look at some examples where good presentation skills are imperative in a business situation. Perhaps you will see yourself in some of these examples.

Example #1

Joe owns a small restaurant. The tenant in the space next door just moved out. Joe decides this would be the perfect opportunity for him to expand his restaurant. In order to do this, however, he will have to obtain a loan so that he can remodel the space and purchase additional equipment. In order to get the loan he needs, Joe is going to have to make a presentation to the loan officer at the bank.

Example #2

Mary is the director of marketing for her company. Recently, her department hired a company to conduct focus group sessions with its customers. The results were surprising. Mary's boss has asked her to make a presentation on the results to the board of directors.

Example #3

Tom manages a small manufacturing plant. Recently, his employees came to him with a way for the company to save money. The only problem is it will require new equipment, which will cost $15,000. Tom must present this proposal to his boss before proceeding.

If you've found yourself in a similar situation, you know just how important good presentation skills are. By reading *Powerful Presentation Skills* you will learn everything you need to know to make you a more powerful, effective communicator.

By honing your presentation skills you will reap many rewards:

- Enjoy an improved vocabulary.

- Develop better reading and listening habits.

- Have a keener interest in things around you.

- Develop an improved ability to think and reason.

- Be more creative.

- Be better able to handle criticism.

- Become a better conversationalist and a more interesting person.

FEAR AND HOW TO OVERCOME IT

If you are afraid of public speaking or making presentations, you're not alone. In fact, one study found that people are more afraid of public speaking than dying.

Most everyone has a desire to be able to speak publicly, but those who fear it can think of more excuses to avoid public speaking than any other activity. Here are some well-used excuses, some of which probably sound familiar to you.

- I get stage fright. (favorite)

- I have never done it before.

- I don't know what to talk about.

- I might forget what I want to say.

- I don't know how to organize my material.

- I might run out of things to say.

- Someone may ask me a question I can't answer.

Some people regard public speaking with such fear that they are even afraid to try it. That's why overcoming fear is the first chapter in this book. Once you get past your fear, the rest will seem easy.

Fear is the most devastating of all human emotions. Man knows no problem like the paralysis of fear. It's the sand in the gears of life.

In order to overcome fear or, as it is commonly referred to, stage fright, you must first understand it — and respect it. More people fail because of fear than inability.

You're Not Alone

So you say, "I can't get up in front of people and speak, I get stage fright." Everybody gets the jitters to some extent. Even professional speakers and presenters experience a certain amount of fear before making presentations.

Eleanor Roosevelt, well into her adult years, was completely terrorized by any thought of making a public address. Others who have admitted to stage fright include Winston Churchill, Helen Keller and Abraham Lincoln. The list is long.

The secret is to learn to control your fear. The individuals just mentioned did, and they all became pretty good speakers.

Identifying Your Fears

Before you can control your fears, you need to identify them. What exactly is it that you are afraid of? Following are some commonly expressed fears.

- I might make a fool of myself.

- I might forget what I am going to say.

- I might begin to stutter or say the wrong thing.

- People may laugh at me.

Analyzing Your Fears

Once you have identified exactly what it is you're afraid of, you can determine if the fear is legitimate. To analyze your fears, ask yourself the following questions:

1. *Is this a rational fear?* For example, examine the fear, "I might make a fool of myself." Ask yourself, "What could I do to make a fool of myself?" Chances are you won't be able to think of a thing. This is an irrational fear. The fear, "I might forget what I am going to say," on the other hand, is indeed a rational fear. You may indeed forget what you are going to say, although this isn't likely if you've rehearsed adequately and have notes.

2. *If this is a rational fear, what is the worst-case scenario?* In the example about forgetting what you are going to say, the worst-case scenario would be that you would indeed forget what you were going to say. Then you would have to refer to your notes.

3. *So what?* In the same example, so what if you have to refer to your notes? Most speakers do at one time or another during their presentations.

By analyzing your fears they become less threatening. This is the first step in helping you to overcome your fear.

Controlling Fear

There are two types of fear: constructive fear and destructive fear. Constructive fear is good. It actually helps you be the best you can be. Destructive fear is bad. It holds you back and can even stop you from trying. The trick is to turn your fear into constructive fear.

Don't let fear paralyze you. Instead, seize every reasonable opportunity to practice your presentation skills. Just like any fear, the best way to overcome the fear of public speaking is to face it head-on.

Facing Fear Head-On

Don't let fear intimidate you. There are four basic facts about fear. Let's examine each.

1. *Fear is inevitable if you are to grow and change.* If you have no fear in your life, you will become stagnant. Anytime you grow and change you experience a certain amount of fear.

2. *The only way to truly overcome a fear is to do whatever it is you fear.* Most things in life aren't nearly as frightening as we make them out to be. Often, we blow them out of proportion. And, the longer we avoid them, the worse they seem. For example, the only way a person can overcome the fear of flying is to take a trip on an airplane.

3. *When it comes to fear, I'm not alone.* Everyone is afraid when they try something new or different. It's human nature. Remembering this fact — that you are not alone — will help.

4. *If you don't face your fear, you will have to live with the underlying fear that comes from helplessness.* If you don't face your fear of public speaking, you will constantly worry that someone will ask you to make a presentation. Then, instead of

suffering through a few minutes of fear, you will have fear hanging over your head for weeks, months or maybe years. Eventually you're going to have to face it, so you might as well get it out of the way.

Stage Fright

The fear a presenter feels right before making a presentation is commonly referred to as "butterflies." Common symptoms of butterflies are sweaty palms, trembling knees and dry mouth. Although these symptoms may cause some initial discomfort, they often go away as you get into your presentation.

The trick in public speaking is to make your stage fright work for you instead of against you. Stage fright in itself is not bad. The best speakers have a healthy respect for it. No matter how many presentations you make, you will always have some stage fright. Use it to help you be your best.

In *Moby Dick,* Captain Ahab declared just before going after the great white whale, "I will have no man in my boat who does not fear a whale."

Be Prepared

The best way to overcome stage fright is to be adequately prepared. Do you recall the motto of the Boy Scouts? It's "Be prepared" — a great standard for life. It is also the way to make stage fright work for you. The more you sweat while preparing for your presentation, the less you'll sweat while making it.

The late Edward R. Murrow, an accomplished speaker, called stage fright the "sweat of perfection." He understood the importance of preparation.

Dale Carnegie earned an international reputation as a speech teacher by helping millions of people. Carnegie once said, "Keep in mind what you have to do when you are afraid. If you are prepared, you will not be fearful." It works for public speaking — and for living, too.

THE BASICS

The best place to learn the basics of good public speaking is in school. But if you are now out of school or haven't yet started, it's no big deal. It is never too late to learn.

Get started—take your first step. Now!

Read About It

There are a number of good books about public speaking. Get several and read them. Each author will emphasize various aspects of speaking in a slightly different way. All will help you.

Recommended books:

- **You Are the Message** by Roger Ailes. New York, NY: Doubleday, 1988.

- **To Meet or Not to Meet** by Karen Anderson. Overland Park, KS: National Press Publications, 1992.

- **Speaker's Edge** by Arthur Bell and Eric Wm. Skopec. Westbury, NY: Asher-Gallant Press, 1988.

- **Get to the Point** by Karen Berg and Andrew Gilman. New York, NY: Bantam Books, 1989.

- **I Can See You Naked** by Ron Hoff. Kansas City, KS: Andrews and McMeel Co., 1988.

- **Osgood on Speaking** by Charles Osgood. New York, NY: William Morrow and Company, 1988.

- **Presentations Plus** by David Peoples. New York, NY: John Wiley, 1992.

Even after reading a book, such as this one, you will sooner or later need "hands-on" experience.

Learning More About Public Speaking

You cannot learn to swim only by reading about it. You must jump in and get wet. There are several places you can go for help.

- *Public and private schools.* Most schools and colleges offer speech instruction. Many are scheduled as evening classes, meeting one to three times a week for the course duration of about three months. Some of them are excellent, some only so-so. If you sign up where instruction is not what it should be, don't stay. Move on and find a class you like.

- *Seminars.* Numerous public and private organizations conduct speech seminars taught by a trained staff. They are usually scheduled as one to three days of intensive study. Enrollment is often limited, allowing good teacher-to-student contact. They are an excellent way to get a quick start and to receive motivation for continued training.

- *Clubs and specialized courses.* There are also clubs and commercial organizations specializing in speech training. Two are described below. Both have been around for a long time and have an excellent reputation. Meetings for each are usually scheduled in the morning or evening for the convenience of working people.

  1. Toastmasters International. A dues-paying club that meets either weekly or bi-weekly. The members teach themselves with guidance from a training manual.

  2. Dale Carnegie Institute. This is a tuition-financed series of rather intensive lessons. The students are taught by an authorized instructor.

- *Tapes.* Excellent public speaking instructional tapes also are available. They are often used as supplemental teaching aids by the organizations previously mentioned.

Getting Practice

There are many places where you can begin speaking. They are all around you. They are golden opportunities for you to not only begin, but also to continue developing your skills. They can be yours simply by volunteering your time.

- *Oral reports at your job.* Start with any assignment you can get—even the most routine and ordinary. Prepare thoroughly; do a good job. You will be surprised how soon the more important speaking offers come.

- *Service clubs.* Volunteer for committee and officer assignments.

- *Fraternal clubs.* Here is a chance to mix your social life with speech training.

- *Civic groups.* Improve your community involvement and speaking skills at the same time.

- *Political and labor organizations.* These groups offer a wide variety of speaking assignments.

- *Church/synagogue.* Opportunities involve things such as lay participation in the religious service, teaching and a host of study groups and committees.

- *Other.* Become actively involved in groups such as garden clubs, scouting, 4–H, PTA, children's sports organizations, stamp clubs, Civil War Round Tables or even Save the Whales. The list is endless.

- *Familiar places.* You might want to start where you feel comfortable—around familiar faces. Fine! Do it. But move on to new and more challenging places as soon as possible.

Don't get caught in a rut!

No one is going to make fun of you. I have never seen an audience snicker or laugh at a speaker who had obviously prepared but was having a tough time. Most people are sympathetic toward a speaker having unexpected trouble.

They will be sitting in their seats silently rooting for you, especially if they know you have prepared and are giving it your best. Audience members will know. You can't fool them!

3

BEFORE ACCEPTING AN INVITATION TO SPEAK

Receiving an invitation to speak is a distinct honor. But with it comes a responsibility. The first question you should ask yourself before accepting a speaking engagement is, "Do I have sufficient time to prepare?"

Preparing a speech can take a lot of time. Don't let anyone tell you differently. Depending on the amount of knowledge you already have about the subject, you will need about an hour of preparation for each minute at the lectern.

Next, ask yourself, "Am I excited about the subject and eager to share what I know with others?" No matter how knowledgeable you are about the subject, if you're not excited about it or about sharing what you know with others, it's going to be difficult to convey the proper enthusiasm to your audience.

If you can't accept a speaking engagement, be ready to suggest someone else who might be able to handle it.

Clarifying the Details

Once you've accepted a speaking engagement, you need to clarify the details. Be sure to get answers to the following questions.

1. How long am I expected to speak?

2. Will the presentation be formal or informal?

3. How large a group will I address? This information will help you determine the type of presentation you make.

4. What is the audience's background?

5. Will there be other speakers? If so, what will they be speaking about? (This will make sure that you don't duplicate material someone else has already covered or material someone else plans to cover after you.)

6. How will the room be arranged?

7. Is an overhead projector, slide projector or other visual aid equipment available?

8. What exactly will I be expected to speak about? For example, if your topic is the company's newest product, what does the group want to know? The benefits of the product? Projected revenues from the product? How the product will be marketed? How to sell the product?

Who's in Your Audience?

After you've gotten the basics, it's important to determine the make-up of the audience that you will address. Knowing this information will not only help you determine what to say, but how to say it. Consider the following groups and the different ways you should address them.

- *Superiors.* If you are addressing a group of your superiors, make your presentation formal, and suggest, don't lecture or dictate. For example, "Given our most recent market analysis, I would recommend the following plan."

- *Peers.* If you are addressing your peers, relate or share information with them. It's also a good idea to involve your peers in the presentation if possible. For example, "Bob, your department did an outstanding job in this area. Can you give us some pointers?"

- *Subordinates.* Use details and demonstrations to relate facts to subordinates. For example, if you are explaining how to prepare departmental budgets to a group of subordinates, have samples available so that they can see how you want it done.

- *Special Interest Groups.* When addressing special interest groups, focus your comments on what matters to them. For example, if you are talking to a group that is concerned about safety on the job, tell them what your company is doing to ensure the safety of its employees. Don't provide the group with a presentation on your newest product or the company's growth. Relate information to these individuals by persuading, convincing or giving opinions.

- *Mixed Groups.* If you are addressing a mixed group, such as peers and subordinates, use a combination of the previously stated techniques in an effort to reach everyone.

What Do They Know?

Once you've determined who is in the audience, you need to determine their level of expertise. In doing so, consider the following questions:

- *Are they informed?* If so, they will be familiar with the topic, so make sure that the information you provide them is not too basic. If they are informed, suggest rather than lecture or teach.

- *Are they uninformed?* If they know nothing about the subject you are presenting, be careful not to talk "over their heads." If you do, they will lose interest and tune you out. If they are uninformed, instruct or teach them.

Before accepting an offer to speak, learn everything you can about your audience, the topic you are to address and the logistics. Knowing this information ahead of time will help you make the best possible presentation. If you don't feel qualified to talk on the topic you've been given, thank the individual and suggest another more qualified person.

Addressing Needs and Wants

Before any presentation, it is imperative that you know and understand the needs of your audience. Let's say you are asked to give a presentation to the Convention and Visitors Bureau on your new hotel. Find out what the individuals want and need to know.

Members of the Convention and Visitors Bureau, for example, won't care about the $50,000 sculpture in the lobby or the type of telephone system that you have. What they will want and need to know is how many rooms the hotel has, the sizes of the meeting rooms, special amenities and the pricing structure.

Before giving the presentation, always find out what the needs and wants of your audience are. Then, develop your presentation around them.

Identify Your Cheerleaders

In every presentation there are people who like and support you or the issue you are presenting. Identify those people — the cheerleaders — who will be in your audience ahead of time and then look for them when you begin your presentation. If you don't know the members of your audience, look for the cheerleaders as soon as you begin your presentation.

In the office, your cheerleaders are easy to spot. These are the individuals who support your ideas and compliment your style. During your presentation, the cheerleaders are those individuals who give their undivided attention, smile at you and maybe even nod in agreement. Playing to the cheerleaders will give you the best possible presentation.

Don't waste your time and energy focusing on the people in your audience who are less receptive. If you do, you will worry so much about why you are not reaching them that you may forget what you were going to say or stumble through your presentation.

4

WHAT TO TALK ABOUT

When deciding what to talk about, you need to consider yourself as well as the audience. Consider the following tips:

- *Stick to something you care about.* It can be a topic you already know about or are willing to learn. There is absolutely no substitute for knowing your subject. You will find it's a good idea to know more about the subject than you can cover during the speech.

- *Believe in what you say.* Avoid topics in which you will make statements of either fact or opinion contrary to what you believe. That's deadly!

- *Don't forget.* Remember the question, "What's in it for me?" The audience is also entitled to ask it. Before you decide what to talk about, discover their wants. What are their interests and needs?

    Is there anything special to them about the speaking situation—the date, the place? Find out and incorporate it into your speech. It will add a nice touch.

Is there a sensitive issue that would cause resentment or misunderstanding? If so, don't talk about it.

- ***Talk about things you and the audience care about.*** Many speeches are boring because they answer questions no one is asking or discuss issues no one is interested in.

- ***Stick to things you have time to cover.*** It is better to talk about something specific than something general. Remember—you should give people something they can use at work or in their daily lives.

- ***Don't spend a lot of time trying to come up with a jazzy title.*** Who cares? No one is going to remember it!

Be on the constant lookout for material. It starts before you are invited to speak and doesn't stop until after the speech. Here are some ways to find new material.

Be a Better Listener

Studies show that the average person speaks about 95 percent of his or her comments and writes only five percent. Somebody must be hearing all this. But are they listening?

Most of us have received very little training in listening—maybe none. Often our listening is disgracefully indifferent and sloppy. Do you suppose we are missing out on something?

Here are a couple of suggestions:

- ***Be selective.*** Not everything you hear is worth listening to. Don't waste your time listening to worthless chatter.

- ***Be attentive.*** Whenever you hear something worthwhile, listen intently and attentively.

To paraphrase Lord Chesterfield's letter to his son, "Blockheads listen to what blockheads say." Listening is a treasure trove for finding speech material. Here are some places to pick up ideas:

1. Casual conversation
2. Radio and TV
3. Civic meetings
4. Service clubs
5. Church/synagogue
6. Other people's speeches
7. Kids

Be a Better Reader

There is tremendous power in the printed word. It has been screened, sifted and has stood the test of time. It's permanent. The best source of things for you to say will be from what you read. Reading is one of the speaker's "tools of the trade." Develop your reading habits and skills in these ways:

- *Learn to read rapidly.* One way is to skim or preview. It gives you a quick, overall view. It helps you decide whether to pass on to something else or go back and pick up important details. This can save you time and improve comprehension of what you read.

- *Pick a quiet place.* When you read, find a quiet place where you are undisturbed and can concentrate. Effective reading is mental work. The last thing you need is noise or interruptions.

- *Read something new.* Read beyond your present knowledge. If you read about only what you know now, your interests will not grow. You grow only when you wrestle with the unfamiliar and partially understood.

You can find an endless variety of literature and written material at libraries, bookstores and your home. Here are sources:

1. Books
2. Encyclopedias
3. Newspapers and magazines
4. Technical, scientific and trade journals
5. Manuals
6. Government and legal documents
7. Religious writings
8. Almanacs

Use Your Experience

Your personal experiences are a valuable source of material. They often will be the reason you have received the speaking invitation. Your experiences add substance and interest to your speech. Sometimes they will be your main source of material. If so, supplement your talk with things you have heard or read.

Be careful to keep the facts of your experience accurate. Don't confuse your opinions with facts.

Use Resources

Become familiar with the public library. It contains an inexhaustible supply of material. The nice thing about the library is that the material is stored in a systematic manner—you can quickly find it. But, you must know the system!

Also, get to know your librarians. They are capable and glad to help you. Most librarians have brochures explaining how to find information. Ask for one. It will show you how to use the card catalogs, the reference indexes and many other facilities for your convenience. It will probably also have a map of the place. You'll need it!

Another resource is to develop your own library. There are some books that you will use so often you may want to buy them. Here are some:

- **Dictionary.** You will be writing most of your speeches. Use the appropriate word and spell it correctly. If you don't own a dictionary, get one.

- **Thesaurus.** This is a very useful book of synonyms and antonyms. Get one of these, too.

- **Encyclopedia.** These are published either as a book or a set of books, giving information on subjects arranged in alphabetical order. Some list general knowledge; others concentrate on a particular field.

- **Dictionary of quotations.** These books are sometimes called Speaker's Handbooks, Stories for Toastmasters, etc. They contain maxims, aphorisms, humorous anecdotes, witty comments, short excerpts from significant literature, etc. They are often compiled by noted editors, writers or speakers. The numerous topics covered are usually carefully indexed to assist you in locating what you need.

- **Almanacs.** These are usually published annually as large paperback books containing statistics on many subjects. They are inexpensive, but contain a great amount of information. If you ever need to know the annual catch of Icelandic cod or the gestation period of the East Indian rhinoceros, then this is the book for you.

Finally, develop a personal notes and file system. Your personal notes can be a valuable source of material. Develop a habit of systematically recording and filing them.

The important thing about making notes is to do it now! Make a note to yourself the moment you hear about something of interest, read about it or when a new idea comes to mind. Unexpected thoughts and ideas are elusive.

They can flee from memory as quickly as they are received, and they may never return!

Your notes will do you no good unless you can quickly find them. Start a note file with a well-planned index system. The standard five-by-eight inch cards and small, desktop filing boxes available at the office supply stores are well suited for your note file.

Be sure your material is accurate. Verify your sources. Have you transcribed it correctly? You have the right to your opinion, but not a right to be wrong with the facts.

Be sure you express the true intent when you summarize others' statements. Quote exactly when you use a direct quotation. If you modify or paraphrase, say so.

Your credibility as a speaker depends upon the credibility of your material!

5

PUTTING IT TOGETHER

Speaking is not writing. Before you start putting your material together, be sure you understand some basic differences between speaking and writing—and between listening and reading. These differences will affect the way you will put your speech together—and the way you will deliver it.

- *Clarity.* Writing is permanent—a sort of congealed communication. The reader can go back and read it again. But the spoken word exists only for the moment. It must be instantly intelligible.

- *Dual communication.* The writer communicates only through the reader's sense of sight. The speaker has access to both the eyes and ears of the audience.

Consequences. Because of these differences, the spoken word:

1. Is more specific than general
2. Is more concrete than abstract
3. Is more illustrative and comparative
4. Has more contrast and suspense
5. Has greater simplicity and rhythm
6. Has greater energy and eagerness
7. Uses a more active voice and more personal pronouns
8. Is more straightforward and climactic

Three Parts of a Speech

Someone once said there are three parts of a speech—the beginning, the end and something in-between. Let us consider them in the order they occur.

The introduction. Here you first meet the audience. It's your big chance to get people's interest and set the tone for the rest of your talk. If ever first impressions are important, this is the place. Here are some suggestions:

- *Acknowledge the chairperson.* Being invited to speak is an honor. It is appropriate to express your gratitude to both the chairperson and the audience. Do it graciously.

- *Pick on yourself.* Sometimes the person introducing you to the audience will make remarks so flowery that they become excessive—to the extent of embarrassment. If you try to deflate the comments, be sure to stick the pin in yourself—not the person who introduced you.

- *Acknowledge the audience.* The audience will appreciate it if members know you are interested in them. Now is a good time to weave into your speech some material of special interest to them—the place, the date or a local person. A little humor here can be good, if done right. (More about trying to be funny later.)

- **Present yourself.** The audience is "sizing you up." Be honest and kind. Establish a friendly and receptive attitude.

- **Announce your topic.** Create immediate audience anticipation. State your main idea clearly and concisely. Do it in a way to arouse interest. Do not tell the title of your speech if the person making the introduction has already done so. Try memorizing this part of your introduction.

The main body. This is where you deliver the "goods." It is the substance of your speech. You develop the theme using facts, examples and illustrations. You continually proceed toward your predetermined conclusion.

During the body of a speech there are four general intentions:

- **To persuade.** This is usually emphasized at a sales meeting.

- **To instruct.** This is usually the easiest—provided you know your subject.

- **To inspire.** You do this at an employee meeting to reduce absenteeism or boost sales.

- **To entertain.** Here you try to be funny. You may think this is the easiest. It's not. Some speakers have never found this out.

The outline. Prepare a plan for the main body of your speech. A topical outline usually works well.

- It will help you say what you want to say. Knowing is not the same as telling.

- It will give continuity and coherence to your speech. This will increase both interest and comprehension by the audience.

Here are some types of outlines:

- *Chronological.* Develop the outline around a chronological series of events.

- *What—how?* Construct the outline by answering "What, why, who, where, when and how?" The introduction may be the appropriate place to present the what and why.

- *Cause and effect.* This may be used effectively when you present consequences of several alternative actions.

- *Others.* You may use combinations of these types. Don't let your outline become complicated. Keep it straightforward, simple and logical.

There are many ways to prepare an outline. Here is one suggestion:

- Write all the points you want to make on three-by-five-inch cards, placing a single point on each card. Carry some cards with you and jot down an idea whenever it comes to mind. This can take several days.

- Sort the cards into piles, each pile containing cards closely related to each other.

- Arrange the piles into a logical sequence.

- Within each pile arrange the cards in a logical and understandable order.

- This is your outline. You can add, change or rearrange.

Conclusion. This is where you clinch the purpose of the speech. You "nail it down" so the audience remembers the main idea. Do it in a climactic and memorable way. This usually will be the part of the speech most remembered.

It is a high achievement to prepare and deliver a speech that is progressively more intense from beginning to end. Don't blow your chance.

Here are some suggestions:

- *Choose your words carefully.* Use them concisely and dramatically to express the important idea the way you want to.

- *Avoid summation.* Do not merely repeat what you have said before.

- *Be brief.* Don't ramble.

- *Memorize it.* Memorize your conclusion. Make it short. You can do it. Say it exactly the way you want to.

- *Say "thank you."* Some speakers believe it is inappropriate to thank the audience at the close of the speech. Do it if you want to. There is nothing wrong with a sincere "thank you"—anytime—anywhere.

Writing Out Presentations

There are two schools of thought about writing out a presentation. One is to write only a topical outline. Get it exactly the way you want it. Become extremely familiar with it—down to the most detailed subheadline. Then when you speak, refer to only the main headings for guidance—from either memory or notes.

The other way is to prepare a complete manuscript. If you are an inexperienced speaker, it is the sure-fire way. It is also a good way to keep improving.

When writing your speech:

- *Stick to your outline.* It will make writing easier.

- *Say what you want to say.* Choose words to accurately express your thoughts.

- *Liven up your talk.* You may want to insert some anecdotes, illustrations or humor to liven up your talk. They should be relevant. Here is where some quotation dictionaries and a good note filing system will come in handy.

- *Keep it simple.* You don't have to use long words or complex phrases to communicate. Read Shakespeare or the Bible to check this out.

- *Avoid jargon.* Use words in the English language. Don't try to be cute.

- *Avoid pretense.* Do not exaggerate. Be yourself.

Edit Ruthlessly

When you are all done, put your written speech aside for a few days. Then pick it up and read it. You will be surprised at how dull some of your "gems" will look.

If any word, phrase, sentence or paragraph does not illuminate your speech, take it out. If there is any doubt—remove it. We all have problems wanting to say it all. When was the last time you heard anyone complain about a speech being too short?

Develop an Agenda

If you are presenting a seminar or a training session, develop an agenda and distribute it at least five working days before your presentation. An agenda will help you keep your presentation on track and help those who need to attend schedule their time. Be sure to include what time you plan to start and end your presentation as well as scheduled breaks.

Using Jokes and Stories

Jokes, humorous stories, epigrams and witty comments or definitions can add clarity and emphasis. They act as the salt and pepper—putting zest and variety into your speech. Carefully sprinkled, they add flavor and refreshment.

Not all speeches need jokes or witty comments. Many inexperienced—and experienced—speakers have the erroneous understanding that humor is frequently needed to keep the attention of the audience.

Abraham Lincoln frequently used humor in conversation. It was always kind. He rarely used it in a public speech. Just reread the Gettysburg Address. King Solomon, whose name is synonymous with wisdom, counseled us, "...there is a time to weep and a time to laugh."

Humor and wit are not substitutes for preparation. Do not plan your speech around jokes and examples.

Carefully prepare your topical outline. Then, while you are writing your speech, insert well-chosen, humorous remarks in selected places. They should be short and relevant to the subject matter. Make your humor, wit and examples support the topical outline.

Use of jokes and humorous stories is often abused. Here are ways to avoid this mistake.

- *Don't be cruel.* Do not hurt anyone. Stay away from jokes about race, religion, sex, mothers-in-law, stuttering, drinking, etc. This type of humor is bound to offend someone in the audience.

- ***You be the "fall guy."*** If the joke does sting, make it on yourself. When telling jokes or making witty comments, it is easier—and better—to have the audience laugh at you than with you.

- ***Avoid anything off-color.*** I should not even have to say anything about this. But many speakers cannot seem to resist telling an off-color joke. It appeals to their vanity. An off-color joke will always bring a few chuckles—it's a sure thing. But, you'll also lose something—respect from some members of your audience. It's not worth the price! Don't do it—ever!

6

VISUAL AIDS

They are often called "visuals." A more accurate term is visual aids. Their purpose is to help the audience understand the spoken word. That's all. Because many speakers don't fully realize this, visual aids often are carelessly prepared and improperly used.

Let's discuss how to prepare and use them.

Informal Presentations

If you are making an informal presentation or speech, you may choose to use flip charts or marker boards. These are best used in small groups and when you want to encourage audience participation. For example, let's say you are meeting with co-workers to determine the company's goals for the coming year. You could use a flip chart or marker board to record what participants see as the main issues the company will face.

To keep the conversation moving, ask a member of the audience to record important points. If you use a flip chart, this information can later be written in summary form and distributed to the participants.

Formal Presentations

Often because of the size of the audience, formal presentations and speeches require more elaborate visual aids. This is mainly so that everyone can see them. Following are some typical visual aids used in formal presentations.

- *Opaque projectors.* These are constructed to directly project pages from a book or report. There are not many of these monstrosities around anymore. They have very poor optical qualities, and they make a great amount of noise.

- *Overhead projectors.* These project a transparency, measuring about eight by 10 inches. Successive transparencies can be overlaid to illustrate a sequence of events. While a transparency is projected, you may write on it with a grease pencil. Nice features! But it's all downhill from there.

  These rather cumbersome machines must be located at the front of the room—between the audience and the screen. They also make considerable noise and emit stray light, which may annoy and distract the audience. Because is virtually impossible to locate the lens perpendicular to the screen, these machines project a distorted image.

  To ensure readability of your transparencies, make sure the letters on the originals are at least one inch high. When making transparencies, place the original on the floor. If you can read it while standing, the type is large enough.

- *35-mm slide projectors.* This equipment is usually available at nearly all auditoriums, meeting centers and other speaking facilities. Standard-sized slides are compatible with projectors representing a wide variety of manufacturers and models.

These projectors are usually equipped with a remote advance/reverse control conveniently operated by the speaker. Optical qualities are excellent! Lenses of various focal length are available, permitting the projector to be located at the back of the room or in a projection booth. A dissolve unit may be operated with two projectors, enabling smooth transition between successive slides.

• *Videotapes.* Videotapes can be used to further explain your subject. For example, if you are speaking about a new treatment for cancer, a videotape showing medical personnel demonstrating these techniques can be helpful. Videotapes, however, should be no longer than 20 to 25 minutes in length. Much longer than that and you lose your audience's attention.

Tips for Preparing Slides and Overheads

If you use a slide projector or overhead projector, the following tips will be helpful.

• Forego the slide if it does not explain the subject better than words.

• Generally use the horizontal format—about five inches horizontal to three-and-a half inches vertical.

• Don't use vertical printing.

• Keep charts and graphs simple. Show only highlights.

• Use the simplest terms—only key words or phrases.

- Use only one idea on each slide.

- Use no more than 40 characters horizontally per line—including spaces.

- Use no more than eight horizontal lines.

- Don't use more than two different type styles on any one visual.

- Use no more than four curves per graph and no date points.

- If possible, use an identical chart layout for all slides in the presentation.

- Use neat draftsmanship.

- Throw away all poorly exposed or unfocused slides.

- Use no more than three colors per slide or transparency.

Tips When Using Visual Aids

It's a team—you and the equipment. Let's talk about the equipment first. Here are things to do before your speech begins.

- Check the length of the extension cords. Do they fit the outlets?

- Be sure the projector works and is set up properly and the lens is focused. When using a videotape, also make sure the tape player is working and that your tape is properly cued up.

- Is there a spare bulb? Does anybody know how to change it and also remove a stuck slide?

- If there is an audio-visual technician to assist you, work out a "slide advance" signal or a signal to start your videotape.

- If there is a speaker's control, become familiar with it.

- Check your slides. Do you have the right ones? Are they in proper sequence and position? Do they advance without sticking?

- Assign someone to control room lights. If lights cannot be dimmed, leave someone in the back of the room to turn them off and on as needed.

- Check the seating. Can everyone see?

- Check the speaker's lectern for everything you will need—pointer and lapel microphone if you must move to the screen.

- Can you read your outline or notes when the lights are dimmed?

Here is a checklist for yourself—things to remember while you speak.

- Do not dim the lights until you actually need the slides, overheads or videotape.

- The projected slide or overhead should show only what you are currently talking about.

- Avoid intermittent use of slides or overheads during your presentation. Arrange your speech so that all of them are shown in an unbroken sequence.

- Look at the audience while the slides or overheads are projected. No one is interested in the back of your head.

- Turn up the lights immediately when finished using your visual aid, then continue your presentation.

A Word of Warning

Visual aids can be tremendously useful for some occasions such as professional presentations, technical briefings, administrative reporting and a host of other instructional speeches. However, when slides or overheads are projected in a darkened room, the speaker immediately becomes isolated from the audience. The same thing happens when a videotape is shown. There is danger of losing some of the close personal relationship so essential to good public speaking.

The gain in communication efficiency by using visual aids may be more imagined than real. All speakers should carefully weigh the advantages and disadvantages. To paraphrase the old merchandising maxim, "Let the speaker beware!"

Handouts and Workbooks

Handouts can be used to highlight information included in your presentation or to provide your audience with additional information. They can either be handed out before or after the presentation or placed on the audience's chairs.

If the information is supplemental, it's best to provide it at the end of the presentation. Otherwise, the audience will be looking through the information while you are trying to speak.

If you are conducting a training session, workbooks can be used to help you illustrate the material you are presenting. Workbooks can include drawings or photographs or tests to help you check the audience's understanding of the material you are presenting.

A Few Reminders

When making an informal presentation, use a flip chart or marker board to encourage audience participation and record important information. When making an formal presentation, opaque projectors, overhead projectors, 35-mm slide projectors or videotapes can add to your presentation. They can help you illustrate or reinforce major points. Before using any visual aid, make sure that it will add to and not detract from your overall presentation.

The best visuals can be spoiled if a carousel of slides is backwards or an overhead transparency is too small to read. Be extremely careful when preparing the visual portion of your presentation. Triple check all equipment right before your presentation.

7

TYPES OF SPEECHES

Now that you have prepared your speech, you need to determine the best way to deliver it. Following is a discussion of several techniques and the pros and cons of each.

The Memorized Speech

One way to deliver your speech is to memorize it, word for word. Many speech books, however, say never to memorize a speech—never! A very dogmatic notion, and some would disagree with it.

Some speeches are suited to memorization, others are not. There are pitfalls and traps, too. If you decide to memorize, be aware of them.

There are some speeches appropriate for memorizing:

- *A short speech.* A speech that lasts from four to six minutes is the easiest to memorize. It's possible, of course, to memorize longer speeches. However, it's best for you to stick to the short ones.

- A speech that will be repeated at other places, to different audiences.

- An especially dramatic or humorous speech—where you desire an unusually close relationship with the audience.

Keep in mind that some very bad things can happen to you while presenting a memorized speech. Your mind might go blank, or you might singsong your way through the entire speech—no tonal variety, no voice inflection, no speech rhythm. Not very impressive—in a favorable way, that is.

Those are only two. But they are enough! So how do you avoid these pitfalls? Knowing the possible problems is a step toward the solution. Here are some suggestions when memorizing a short speech.

- Divide your speech into 10 to 15 small, logical parts—each topic or set of closely-related sentences and portions that are adjacent to illustrative material.

- Then slightly rework the end of each part so it has a key word or phrase closely related to the general idea of the next part.

- These key words will automatically get you started on the next part.

- Start memorizing early. At first, concentrate on only recalling the words.

- A few days before the speech, begin practicing with proper inflection, pauses, etc.

• Prepare a small slip of paper listing, in chronological order, the key words to successive parts of the speech. It is your hand-held "prompter" just in case you need it. You'll feel better having the insurance. No one will even know you have it.

The Read Speech

With this way of delivering a speech there are few, if any, deviations of the spoken word from the printed manuscript. Additions, deletions or changes from the manuscript are seldom made and have minor importance. What the audience hears is, essentially, what the speaker is reading, word for word, from the manuscript.

There are occasions when reading the manuscript is an appropriate way to present a speech. Here are some of them:

• When the speech involves unusually important and sensitive issues requiring exact wording

• When exact details of events, dates or policies are important

• When advance copies of the speech have been released

• When the speaker must adhere to a tight time schedule

This may seem a safe way to deliver a speech. After all, what could go wrong? But often our dangers in life are where they are least expected. There are some things that can go wrong.

• The audience members may immediately sense the presence of the manuscript. If they do, a barrier will go up!

• You might present such excessive detail that you lose the audience. This commonly happens when professional papers or technical reports are involved.

- You may unconsciously begin to read in a monotone voice—no voice inflection or rhythm. The audience will fall asleep!

- You may feel a compelling need to ad lib a few unprepared remarks to break the grinding monotony. This often causes a severe case of "foot-in-the-mouth" disease.

- You may get into the habit of using reading a speech as a crutch—depending on it to avoid confronting the audience.

If you do decide to read your speech, here are some suggestions for doing it effectively.

- Reading an important speech—or parts of a speech—can lend importance to the occasion. But don't abuse it.

- Prepare the manuscript in double-spaced, large-type print. Underline key sentences. Make it easy to read.

- Read the final lectern manuscript many times. Have it almost memorized.

- Look at the audience while you speak. Glance at the manuscript only occasionally to prompt yourself or to directly read significant but brief details.

- Speak in a natural manner. Avoid the sleep-inducing "reader's voice."

If you do it right, the audience will hardly know you are reading the speech.

The Extemporaneous Speech

The term "extemporaneous" is often confused with the term "impromptu." An extemporaneous speech is delivered using notes and according to a carefully predetermined plan. However, the speaker is so familiar with the plan that little, if any, visible reference is made to it during the presentation.

A major characteristic of extemporaneous speaking is its naturalness. It conveys the personality of the speaker to the audience. Consequently, the audience becomes more attentive and receptive. Tests have shown an audience retains about 35 percent more from an extemporaneous speech than from any other.

The extemporaneous speech is suited for all occasions. It has universal application. With the exception of short, memorized portions from the main body, your material can usually be most effectively presented in the extemporaneous manner.

Even national government leaders—accomplished speakers—often read word for word from a TelePrompTer or cue cards to give the illusion of an extemporaneous speech.

Because of fear, many speakers avoid extemporaneous speaking in favor of reading the speech. The mere mention of speaking from only notes causes terror and trembling.

Hear Eleanor Roosevelt: "I believe anyone can conquer fear by doing the things most feared—provided he keeps doing them until getting a record of successful experiences."

Here are some suggestions for speaking extemporaneously.

- Prepare a written manuscript.

- Read it over many times. Become thoroughly familiar with it.

- Prepare a speaking outline consisting of the main speech topics, including brief material you want to quote directly. There are two ways to do this.

- Use standard eight-and-a-half by eleven inch paper or, for convenience at the lectern, use five-by-eight-inch cards; or
- Make a chronological list of the main topics on small, palm-held cards. You will greatly appreciate this method at those unexpected times when a speaker's lectern is unavailable.

- Memorize the main topics of the outline.

- Practice delivering the speech using the outline only as a prompter. Check to make sure you stay close to the working manuscript.

A Combination of Ways

Often there are occasions when memorization and reading can be effectively combined with the extemporaneous method. Memorization of brief passages requiring the exact, predetermined wording can achieve the extemporaneous effect yet retain the preciseness of thought. Also, purposefully reading short, important passages can lend emphasis and dramatic effect to the extemporaneous speech.

The Impromptu Speech

The impromptu speech is presented with no predetermined detailed plan or outline. The speaking occasion arises unannounced and probably unexpectedly. So, the ability to speak in the impromptu manner is a tremendous asset.

This does not imply that the capable impromptu speaker is either uninformed or unprepared. She or he arrives equipped with the tools of prior experience, listening, reading and thinking about the subject.

You acquire expanded knowledge and interests as you improve your ability to organize your thoughts for formal public speaking. While doing so, you can also enhance your skills for impromptu speaking.

Get into the habit of anticipating the opportunity for the short impromptu speech or comment.

Before the occasion for the speech arises, mentally form a short plan.

1. State the main idea
2. Develop the argument.
3. State the conclusion.

Then, when the "unexpected" occasion does arrive, stand and concisely present the impromptu speech from your mental outline.

Do some thinking at your seat. Don't leave it all to thinking on your feet. If you have nothing to say, don't stand up.

The Entertaining Speech

A few words now about the humorous speech.

Here is where you entertain—only. You are not trying to inform or save souls. There is no introduction, main body or conclusion. This type of speech is unique—it's in a class by itself.

Mark Twain, an accomplished humorous speaker, had a talent for stretching out one humorous incident for the duration of a highly entertaining speech. Other humorous speakers, such as Bob Hope, have a "machine gun" delivery—rapidly firing off salvos of one-liners, short jokes and witty comments about a variety of subjects. Others develop their highly humorous speech around a definite topic. There is no set pattern for a successful humorous speech.

If you do decide to give a humorous speech, here are some tips:

- *Keep your first attempts short.* (And remember, you'll make it without notes!)

- *Select your jokes carefully.*

- *Arrange the anecdotes, jokes, witty comments and other narratives in an order so that one leads to the other.* This will do two things:

  - Your speech will flow in an easy and natural order.
  - It will help you to remember what comes next.

- *Practice until it all comes easily.*

- *Be yourself.* Don't try to imitate other noted comedians.

- *Be flexible.* Save an unusually good story for last. Don't hesitate to go to it sooner than usual if things aren't going right.

8

SPEAKER'S STYLE

"The way of speaking I love is natural and plain—a sinewy way of
expressing one's self. It is free from affectation."
—Michel De Montaigne

A mannerism is specific. A speaker's style is the general way of
selecting, using, expressing and emphasizing words. It is distinct from the
idea of the speech.

We often regard style in terms of a current fashion. Not so for style in
public speaking. Here it has a more lasting quality, a permanence. It is often
the characteristic or quality most identified with the speaker.

The speaker's personality is reflected in the style of delivery. You cannot
mask your personality from your speaking style. Eventually, your personality
will be revealed. This gives a clue on how to develop an effective and
pleasing style of speaking.

Identifying Your Style

There is no single correct style. Styles vary widely among successful speakers. Here are examples of accomplished speakers having widely differing styles. In each case, the style reflects a measure of the character of the speaker.

- *Accessibility.* Charles de Gaulle, the French national leader, at all times maintained a style of regal aloofness from his audiences and devoted following. U.S. President Harry Truman, on the other hand, spoke with extreme candor and frankness.

- *Speed.* A characteristic of the Reverend Billy Graham's effective style is a rapid speaking rate, conveying a sense of urgency to his message. The late Senator Everett Dirksen spoke with unusual deliberation and exactness.

- *Word selection.* William Jennings Bryan, the "man with the golden tongue," had a style for flamboyant expression using colorful phrases and unusual similes. Abraham Lincoln invariably conveyed his ideas with well-chosen, unadorned, simple words.

- *Humility.* A distinguishing feature of Booker T. Washington was extreme modesty and humility. The style of General Douglas MacArthur emphasized confidence and assurance to such an extent that humility was lacking.

Developing Your Speaking Style

This is where the term "art" comes from. Often art is regarded as an inherent, not an acquired talent. For some forms of art this is true. Speaking style is an art, but it can be developed. Here are some thoughts about developing a pleasant speaking style.

- *Enduring ideas.* Your style should reflect the way you can do the most. Forget about immediate rewards. Lincoln's debates with Stephen Douglas did not get him a seat in the U.S. Senate. But Lincoln is now remembered for greater goals. Both Hitler and Mussolini had a dynamic speaking style—but they didn't last. Become interested and involved in enduring ideas and values.

- *Sincerity.* Effective speech must come from one's convictions. Nothing replaces sincerity. Will Rogers was one of America's most beloved humorists, a sincere, funny man. He loved people, and he meant it when he said, "I never met a man I didn't like." His audience understood.

- *Enthusiasm.* Become genuinely interested in what you talk about. Ralph Nader, an effective speaker, violates many "rules" of speaking. He walks to the lectern carrying an outlandish armload of books, rolled-up newspapers and reports to support his ideas. He is always enthusiastic about his urgent message; enthusiasm can't be turned on and off like a faucet.

- *Being yourself.* You are free to use any style, provided it is natural, sincere and effective. But you must be yourself. Be honest, loving and sympathetic. You should never appear clever and make a show of your talents. Applause will come unsolicited from those who know what to applaud.

    Don't try to be someone else by adopting a style you admire—develop your own style.

- *Improving yourself.* Don't remain the same person tomorrow as you are today. Discover where your shortcomings are. Continually repair them; study other speakers. Improve yourself—improve your style.

9

REHEARSING YOUR PRESENTATION

In 600 B.C., Periander of Corinth said, "Practice is everything." More than 2,500 years later, Ralph Waldo Emerson put it in a slightly different way: "Practice is nine-tenths." Is practice really all that important? Yes!

Effective public speakers universally recognize the value of practicing and rehearsing. It is a vital part of speech preparation. In fact, experts suggest that you spend half of your preparation time practicing. For example, if you spend six hours researching and organizing your material, you should spend six hours rehearsing.

Winston Churchill had a love affair with the English language. Few men have appreciated the value of the spoken word more or have been more skilled in its use. His colorful and dramatic career was highlighted by his zeal for writing and speaking effectively. Although he was a very skilled speaker, he never abandoned his self-imposed rule of carefully rehearsing every speech.

Reasons to Rehearse

There are many reasons for you to rehearse the delivery of your presentation.

- To help you detect "bugs" in your manuscript, such as:

  - Grammatical violations, poor word selection or incoherent sentence structure
  - Illogical organization
  - Inadequate information or excessive detail
  - Poor logic and reasoning

- To help you look and feel more comfortable

- To improve your vocal variety and speech phrasing

- To improve the effectiveness of your gestures

- To reduce annoying mannerisms so the right words come out naturally and pleasantly

- To avoid mispronounced words

- To help you use your visual aids effectively

- To help you finish on time

- To stop you from adding any new but bad ideas

How to Rehearse

The first thing you need to do is to stop feeling self-conscious about rehearsing. This prevents many speakers from practicing. They think they will feel "silly," so they avoid ever trying.

Next, you need to adopt an inflexible rule about its urgency. Repeatedly rehearse every speech. Start early so you have the opportunity to do it many times—at least every day for the week before the speech.

Use the same words and gestures you will use at the speech. Do it exactly as you will when speaking.

Rehearse in front of a mirror. Watch yourself carefully.

Videotape your presentation or give it in front of a small group of people. If you videotape it, answer the following questions when you review the tape.

- Did you appear in control?

- How was your posture?

- Did your gesturing seem natural?

- Did your visuals complement your presentation?

- How was your eye contact? Did you look out at your audience (the camera)?

- Did you smile and appear relaxed?

- How was your speech? Did you talk too fast or too slow? Was your volume too soft or too loud?

- Did you discover any negative speech mannerisms such as repeatedly saying "okay" or "um"?

- Did you use pauses effectively?

Go through the entire speech each time you rehearse. Duplicate the speaking situation as closely as possible. Continue to rehearse your presentation until you have corrected all of your shortcomings and feel confident. Then, visualize yourself successfully making your presentation. Continue to use this visualization technique daily to help build your confidence.

If you give your presentation to a group of friends or peers, ask them to critique your performance. Accept criticism graciously and encourage them to be open and honest with you.

Talk to the Tombstones

An ambitious young person once asked British Prime Minister Benjamin Disraeli what course of study to take to become a speaker. Disraeli asked, "Is there a graveyard near your house?" "Yes," was the reply. "Then," said Disraeli, "I recommend you visit it early in the mornings and practice to the tombstones."

Again, practice makes perfect.

10

JUST BEFORE IT BEGINS

What you do during the last 30 minutes before the program starts can greatly affect how your speech goes. You have worked so hard up to now in all phases of preparation, it would indeed be unfortunate to neglect these vital last few moments. Here are some tips to make everything run smoothly.

- Arrive at least 30 minutes before the program begins.

- Meet the chairperson or whomever will introduce you. If you have not done so already, give that person a brief written statement about yourself.

- If copies of your written speech are available, ask the person introducing you to make that announcement.

- Tell that same person if there will be a discussion after the speech.

- Have a brief and cordial conversation with others on the program.

- Check facilities at the lectern. Stand behind it. Become familiar with it.

- Walk throughout the room and sit in various chairs to get a feel for how the members of your audience will feel. Are there any pillars that will block their view? If so, try to have the chairs rearranged.

- If a portable lectern is to be brought in, find out about it— where will it be located?

- If a public address system is available, use it unless it is defective or the room is small.

- Use a lapel microphone, if available.

- Try out the acoustics of the room with the public address system. Pre-set the volume. Find out if someone is assigned to adjust the controls.

- Pour yourself a couple of glasses of water and place them at the lectern.

- If you will be using slides or other visual aids, check all the things about them we have previously discussed.

- Check your appearance—how do you look?

- Triple-check all equipment.

- Check the temperature of the room. Is it too warm or too cool? Find out how to adjust the thermostat or make sure that someone knows how to do it.

- Find a quiet place to concentrate on your speech for a few minutes. Take a few deep breaths and relax. You're ready to go.

If you leave the room, be careful where you go. Several years ago I went to a nice quiet room. Soon a lady came in. The conversation went like this:

Lady: "Who are you?"

Me: "I am tonight's speaker. I just came in here to think about my speech."

Lady: "Do you always get nervous like this?"

Me: "Nervous? Who's nervous? I am not nervous."

Lady: "Say, mister, if you are not nervous, what are you doing here in the ladies rest room?"

Tips to Help You Relax

Arriving early and triple-checking all of the details is the first step in helping you feel confident that your presentation will go well. If you still feel a little nervous, however, try some of the following tips to help you relax.

- Take several deep breaths.

- Read through your presentation.

- Sit in a quiet area and visualize yourself giving a good presentation.

- Use "self-talk" to tell yourself that you have adequately prepared and will do a good job. Then go out and do it!

11

DELIVERING YOUR PRESENTATION

The audience is both listening and watching. The things they see are not in the manuscript. Some of the things they hear may not be there either. Both listening and watching are important—yet you, as the speaker, may be unaware of either their existence or their consequences.

Appearance

Appearance alone does not make the speaker. But it will pay to look your best. Dress appropriately for the occasion. Be careful about casual clothes. You will never go wrong dressing up.

Be neat. Shine your shoes. Comb your hair. Check your make-up. Are your clothes pressed? You get the idea!

Body Language

Studies show that body language accounts for 55 percent of total communications. When making a presentation, consider the following:

- *Use good posture.* Stand erect—don't slouch. This not only looks good, but it will improve your voice.

- *Don't lean on the lectern.* It makes you look tired, like you need a rest.

- *Don't play with jewelry, your hair or clothing.* Doing so will make you appear nervous.

- *Walk around naturally, don't pace.* If you choose to walk around the room while you are talking, move around casually. Doing so will help you maintain your audience's attention.

- *Use facial expressions.* The audience will be looking at your face most of the time. Your audience receives your message from your face. Two thousand years ago the Roman poet Ovid wrote, "A pleasing countenance is no small advantage." He later was run out of the country—but that's another story.

What the Audience Will See

Also consider what the following body language says about you.

- *Smile.* A cheerful face on the speaker will bring cheerful faces to the audience. It's difficult for a smiling audience to be either inattentive or disinterested.

- *Eyes.* Look at the audience. Get into the habit of directing your attention for brief periods to all sections of the audience. If you look at people , they will look at you.

- *Your hands.* No one has a "hand problem" during normal conversation—we use our hands to gesture in a natural way. We are not even aware of them.

Gesturing

A good speaker automatically delivers a well-rehearsed speech in a manner similar to normal conversation—naturally and effortlessly. A speaker should not regard "hands" as a problem, but use natural hand gestures to supplement the easy flow of speech. Rehearsing pays!

Male speakers should purposefully avoid putting their hands into their pockets. This may take considerable resolve. Merely having your hands in your pockets does not distract the audience, but repeatedly putting your hands in your pockets can cause a distraction.

There are two things you should never do with your hands.

1. Don't pick your nose.
2. Don't scratch where it itches.

Your Voice

There is a widespread need for a thorough cultivation of the voice. It is surprising how few speakers give real attention to this important subject. Here are some suggestions on using your voice at the lectern.

- *Speak up.* No one in the audience should have to strain to hear. Nor should you have to shout.

- *Use good diction.* Enunciate your words clearly so the audience can understand. Don't slur your words or mumble. Don't try to speak while chewing gum or smoking.

- ***Breathe normally.*** Your sentences in ordinary conversation are short. You complete them before running out of breath. Remember that when writing your speech.

- ***Speak pleasantly.*** This means using pleasing tonal variety, voice inflection and speech rhythm. Your voice should sound natural, a characteristic of normal conversation. Again, rehearsing pays.

- ***Improve voice quality.*** Many speakers, through habit, tighten the mouth and throat muscles, causing the voice to rise to an unnatural and unpleasant higher pitch. There is a tendency to do this during momentary nervousness at the beginning of a speech. Speech therapists can help those having a persistently unpleasant pitch.

- ***Don't rush.*** Don't speak too fast. Most good speakers say about 100 words per minute. Remove some material if your speech will run long.

- ***Drop the pitch of your voice.*** Doing so will give the impression of authority and power.

- ***Treat a dry throat.*** Take a small sip of room-temperature water when you first feel it. Bite your tongue lightly if you have no water. Avoid cold liquids and caffeine. They will make your vocal cords contract.

Speech Mannerisms

A mannerism is a habit. It's like a rope—we weave a strand each day, and soon we cannot break it.

It is just as easy to form a good habit as a bad one. Also, it is as hard to break a bad habit as a good one. The trick is to get the good ones and keep them.

There are hundreds of different speech mannerisms—some are good, some are bad. Both are used unconsciously. But even good ones can become bad when used excessively. Everyone remembers the bad ones—they distract and annoy the audience.

Below is a list of negative speech mannerisms. Work on eliminating these from your repertoire.

- *"Uh-uh-uh."* Many speakers have an uncontrollable urge to always have a sound pouring from their mouths. Silence is unbearable. This mannerism becomes a "filler" before the next idea comes or even between each sentence! This is an extremely tough one to break.

- *"You know."* This one is done for the same reason as "uh." Avoid them both.

- *Weaving back and forth.* This is a form of nervousness, like jiggling your foot or cracking your knuckles. It's extremely distracting. Soon the audience becomes worried you will fall over or break your hand.

- *Licking your lips.* There are many facial mannerisms like this: grimacing, head jerking, eye blinking and all the other distractive variations. When these nervous habits do not exist during ordinary conversation, better speech preparation is the sure cure.

- *Repeated meaningless hand gestures.* Variety and spontaneity of hand gestures can lend dramatic emphasis.

Some speakers limit postures to one or two repeated movements. Anticipated, unnatural and inappropriate, they become an embarrassment.

- *Playing with things.* Toying and fiddling with handy items such as eyeglasses, pencils, keys or note cards can distract audience members. Soon they are not listening. Do not even pick things up if you can't control yourself.

Building Rapport

An essential feature of any good presentation is to establish and maintain a personal and cordial relationship with the audience. By building rapport with your audience up front, you will convey that you truly believe what you are about to say, and, as a result, the audience will respond more positively to you.

Following are some tips to help you build rapport with your audience.

- *Ask questions.* Begin your speech by asking the group to respond to a question. This gets everyone involved from the very beginning. For example, if you are giving a presentation on computer skills you might ask, "How many of you have ever used a computer before?"

- *Avoid "me."* In a presentation, people want to know how what you are talking about is going to affect them. If you use "me" or "I" too much, they will tune you out. In other words, instead of saying, "This is how I want you to do this," say, "You will find it easiest to do it this way."

- *Thank or compliment the audience.* Begin by thanking your audience for asking you to speak. Or start your presentation with a compliment such as, "During the first quarter of this year you have done an outstanding job. Today we need to talk about what you will need to do to meet your goals for the rest of the year." When making compliments, be sincere. If you're not, your audience will see right through you.

- *Bring up a non-related subject of mutual interest.* For example, if most of the members of your audience enjoy baseball, you might start your presentation by talking casually about the game the night before.

Building Credibility

As a presenter, it is imperative that your audience view you as a credible source. Following are some tips to help you build credibility with your audience.

- *Begin your presentation on time.* By doing so you are telling your audience members that you respect their time.

- *Be well prepared.* There's no substitute for preparation. If you are not well prepared, your audience will pick up on it immediately and you will lose credibility.

- *Answer questions directly.* Don't get sidetracked. When an audience member asks you a question, give a complete but succinct response.

- *If you don't know an answer to a question, say so.* Don't pretend. Simply say you don't know the answer, but that you will be happy to get back to the individual. Then, make sure that you do.

- *Use specific examples.* Specific examples will help you get your point across and help build your credibility.

- *Remain in control.* Regardless of what happens, stay in

control. Don't let interruptions of any kind get you off course or fluster you.

- ***End your presentation on time.*** Just as starting your presentation on time gives you credibility, so does ending your presentation on time. If you have a question-and-answer session that is running long, end on time and tell the audience that anyone is invited to stay afterward and ask questions one-on-one.

The 10 Most Common Mistakes Speakers Make

There is no such thing as a natural speaker. But, if you prepare, practice and avoid some common pitfalls, you can become an effective presenter. Following are 10 of the most common mistakes presenters make. Keep them in mind and avoid them.

1. ***Lack of preparation.*** Too often a potentially good presentation is ruined because a speaker doesn't take the time needed to prepare. Even if you're asked to give just a short five-minute presentation, your preparation and practice are vital.

2. ***Poor use of visual aids.*** Visuals should enhance your presentation, not detract from it. If you use visual aids, make sure that they add something to your presentation.

3. ***Inappropriate humor.*** When used appropriately, humor can add zest to a presentation. But off-color jokes or those that might be viewed as derogatory by a segment of your audience will doom your presentation.

4. ***Inappropriate dress.*** A wild tie or bright skirt, while appropriate for some occasions, probably will be distracting during a presentation. Your best bet is to dress conservatively so that your

audience pays attention to what you're saying and not what you're wearing.

5. *Not knowing the audience.* Be sure to find out the make-up of your audience. If your presentation is too basic for your audience or if it is too technical or "over their heads," audience members will turn you off.

6. *Non-functioning or malfunctioning visual aids.* If you plan to use visual aids, make sure they work ahead of time. Malfunctioning equipment will distract you, and your audience will lose interest.

7. *Starting or ending a presentation late.* Like you, the members of your audience have time constraints. Respect them.

8. *Using a monotone voice.* No matter how good your material, if you talk in a monotone, you will lose your audience.

9. *Trying to present too much material in too little time.* If you don't have enough time to present all of the material, carefully see what you can cut back on or cut out. It's better to give your audience a shorter version that everyone will understand than to rush through your presentation and leave everyone confused.

10. *Not clarifying the topic.* If you don't clarify the topic ahead of time, you may find yourself speaking on a topic that isn't of interest to your audience.

12

IS ANYONE LISTENING?

Occasionally a speaker may see unmistakable signs of audience disinterest and inattention. If it is widespread, the audience probably has justifiable complaints, such as:

- The speech is disorganized—hard to follow.

- They cannot hear; the speaker is talking too fast.

- It's boring.

- The speaker is not interested in it, either.

- It's too long.

These are sure signs of poor speech preparation. There is little a speaker can do in the middle of a speech to correct this oversight. Impromptu remarks and off-the-cuff comments usually increase the trouble. The best immediate solution is to quickly wind it up and sit down.

Use this bad experience to learn a most valuable lesson about the importance of speech preparation.

Handling Unexpected Disturbances

Sometimes when you are delivering a well-prepared speech to an interested and appreciative audience, an unexpected disturbance may occur. The extent of distraction to the audience depends upon the persistence of the disturbance and how the speaker handles it.

Several types of disturbances, although unplanned, are rather common. Their destructive consequences can be reduced if the speaker has a general, predetermined policy for handling them. The unexpected disturbance is then no longer a surprise.

There is no single correct way to handle each type. Details of each situation vary. Also, the appropriate way to handle them will depend upon the personality and style of the speaker.

Here are some general rules:

- Don't hurt anyone. Be kind.

- Make the joke on yourself when you use humor to smooth things over. For example, in the middle of a presentation, a beeper went off in the front row. It could be heard throughout the room. Without missing a beat, the speaker said, "Please don't leave—you're the only one who's laughing at my jokes."

- Resist the urge to put someone down.

There are countless distracting surprises that can come unannounced. Here are suggestions for some of them:

- *The unfriendly audience.* You may face an unfriendly audience. This may be a surprise or you may have anticipated it. Either way, your best approach is to emphasize points of agreement. Never become argumentative. You will not convert anyone.

- *People leaving.* Some in the audience may come in late, move around or leave early. Ignore them if they are small in number. Don't admonish anyone. Terminate your speech early if the situation takes on the proportions of a stampede or a mass exodus.

- *Photographers.* They will be down in front between you and the audience. All they want is a picture of you "in action"—mouth open with an outstretched arm. Help them. Hold the pose momentarily during your normal speech delivery. Then they will be gone.

- *Pause—a long one.* Sometimes, in spite of all your preparation, memory momentarily fails. It may seem like eternity. It's not. Here is where a little self-humor can turn a "disaster" into an asset. For example, tell your audience your biggest mistake tonight was when you got up out of your chair. You will have time to remember what to say while people are laughing. There are jokes you can tell on yourself to cover any situation. Or, if you are making an informal presentation, ask if anyone has questions. This will give you time to compose your thoughts.

- *Excessive drinking.* If there is a social hour before the program, you may encounter people who have had too much to drink. If you think there will be a problem, politely mention this to the chairperson or another in charge. Let someone else handle this potential source of trouble. Never compete with someone who has been drinking.

- *The heckler.* You hear a lot about hecklers. They are not as prevalent as you might think. If you ever have this problem, never respond to the taunts. Stay cool. Keep poised. If it persists, calmly sit down.

- *Mistakes.* Even accomplished speakers make mistakes.
  Things like a mispronounced word, forgetting a name,
  using the wrong name, notes falling off the lectern, slides
  upside down—the possibilities are endless. Have a
  repertoire of humorous comments and stories specifically
  appropriate for several common, unplanned situations. The
  spontaneity of these remarks can be a highlight of your
  speech.

- *When someone falls asleep.* If people in the audience
  begin to doze, walk slowly toward them while increasing
  your voice. Don't look directly at them, but stay in their
  general vicinity for a few moments. By doing this you will
  recapture their attention without embarrassing them.

The ability to remain flexible in your speech does not imply that you shouldn't be thoroughly prepared. Flexibility is an added dimension of preparation—be prepared to be flexible.

The ability to smoothly modify, delete or add material to a well-prepared speech while at the lectern is a skill achieved with experience...and no small amount of planning and preparation.

Planning for Attention Span

In any presentation, audiences will tend to come and go mentally. Although you can't control the fact that people's minds will drift occasionally, you can, to some degree, control their attention spans.

Following is a description of four attention spans you might want to incorporate into your speech or presentation.

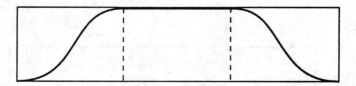

• *Instructional.* This is the type of attention span you want to plan for if you are training or explaining something. Ease into your topic, capture your audience's attention and then gradually let people go. This can be done by including a review or summary at the end of your presentation. Instructional presentations generally are two hours or shorter in length.

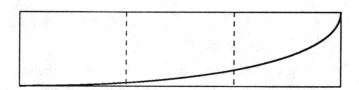

• *Motivational.* This is the type of attention span you should plan for if you are giving a motivational presentation such as a sales pep talk. Start out slow and end strong so that your audience leaves geared up and ready to go.

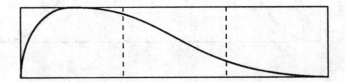

- *Keynote.* If you are going to have a keynote speaker, you want your audience's attention to be strongest during that person's remarks. In this instance, plan for high energy at the beginning when your keynoter will be speaking and then gradually bring the presentation to a close.

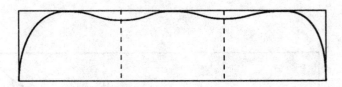

- *Drift.* For longer presentations, those that last two hours or longer, plan for your audience's attention to go up and down. You can do this by bringing the energy level up and then letting it drift back down. Ease out with a review or a summary of what's been covered.

13

BRINGING YOUR PRESENTATION TO A CLOSE

Questions and Answers

Questions after a presentation are evidence of an attentive audience. A question-and-answer period can contribute to the speech—clarifying and expanding points of special interest to the audience.

Some speakers like to have a question-and-answer period. The decision to accept questions is up to the speaker. It is important to be so thoroughly informed that you can handle any question on the subject. An important ingredient of being informed is to know what is not known.

How to do it. If you, as a speaker, decide to answer questions, here are some suggestions:

- Notify the chairperson about your decision before the speech.

- After the conclusion of your speech, have the person in charge announce that you will answer questions and how much time will be allowed. For example, "We have about 15 minutes. Ms. Smith will now answer any questions you have."

The question-and-answer format will depend upon the size of the audience.

1. If the room doesn't require a public address system, have the questioner stand and directly ask you the question. Politely stress the need for brevity. Repeat the question to ensure that all heard.

2. If it's a large audience, suggest that questions be written on paper furnished by ushers after you have finished. These are to be quickly collected and given to the person in charge who will sort them and state selected, representative questions.

After each question is asked, state the answer concisely and briefly.

Don't argue with a contentious questioner—it's not a debate. If she or he persists, politely list points of agreement and move on.

If you do not know the answer, say so. Offer to meet the questioner afterward to obtain his or her name and address for replying later.

Terminate the session if the hour is getting late—even if the discussion is lively and enthusiastic. Some people will want to go home. Announce that you will remain afterward to continue the discussion.

Evaluations

Asking the audience to complete evaluation forms will help you plan future presentations. Evaluations can either be formal and prepared ahead of time or you can simply ask your audience to jot down their comments on three-by-five-inch cards.

Ask your audience to evaluate the following:

- The content of your presentation

- Your presentation style

- The facility/room where the presentation was held

- The visuals (if used)

You might also want to ask audience members if they would recommend the program to a friend. This will tell you how they really felt.

This information will help you determine your strengths and weaknesses. Use it to help you plan future presentations.

14

AFTER IT'S ALL DONE

All done. The speech is delivered! Here's what happens now:

- You will soon receive a letter from the chairperson or someone else in attendance. It will be a "thank you" letter, kindly expressing appreciation for the speech. A nice gesture.

- Another nice gesture would be for you to mail a reply. Nothing fancy, just a short, sincere acknowledgment of his or her thanks is always in style.

Evaluate Yourself

We hear much about the value of experience. It is often regarded as the ultimate standard for qualification. But, experience has no standard. Ten years of experience might be merely one year's experience repeated 10 times. The first thing we need to do is identify our mistakes.

You probably have a pretty good idea of how your speech went. However, we are frequently deceived by our own thoughts about ourselves. Here are some suggestions about asking, receiving and using criticism.

- Ask individuals whose opinions you trust what they thought of your presentation. Do it soon afterward, while it is still fresh in their minds.

- Request criticism on all aspects of the presentation: appropriateness of topic, comprehensiveness of material, clarity of organization and delivery.

- Receive all comments in a receptive and gracious manner. Never question their validity.

- Later, evaluate the criticism. Do it honestly and objectively.

- Incorporate corrective action into future speeches. Don't keep making the same mistakes. Be determined to improve with each successive speech.

- Make notes on techniques that did and did not work.

If you don't know how to receive and use criticism, now is the time to start.

After you've asked others for their opinions, critique your performance, your visuals and the facilities. Write a report and review it before you make your next presentation. In doing so, ask yourself the following questions:

- How did I feel before the presentation? (If you were nervous, note what you did to relax yourself.)

- How did I feel once I got into the presentation? (If you were nervous, note why. For example, you didn't feel adequately prepared, the room wasn't arranged as you had anticipated, etc.)

- How do I feel I came across? Why do I feel that way? (For example, I believe my presentation was well received because several people asked pertinent questions afterwards.)

- How were my visuals? Is there anything I would have done differently?

- How was the meeting space? Was there anything about it I didn't like? If you note what you didn't like, it will help you make changes next time.

- Was the room comfortable?

Store your critique with your presentation materials. Then, next time you are asked to speak, review your critique to help you do an even better job.

Save Everything

Save all your manuscripts and all your resource notes, too. They will be a valuable source of material for new speeches.

Be very careful about giving the same speech again. Even better—just don't do it. You should be a better speaker tomorrow than you are today.

Let's improve ourselves. We cannot remain stationary. We either go forward or backward.

Review Your Practice Video

If you videotaped your rehearsed presentation or if a videotape is available of your actual presentation, study it carefully. Look for things you would have done differently and note them for the next time.

Confidence Is a Slippery Pal

Confidence is essential to successful achievement of any activity. Speaking is no exception.

Confidence is invariably a constructive and stimulating force during the first few successful speeches. Here confidence is beneficial—it's healthy.

Frequently something soon happens to the successful speaker. Buoyed by a consistent history of success, a false confidence can slowly emerge. Gradually success in speaking verbally is perceived more as a result and less as a goal. Preparation slacks off. A few attempts to "wing it" are not noted for success. But neither are they recognized as failures. Gradually the "bottom drops out." The speaker eventually loses interest—gradually abandoning the endeavor altogether.

To paraphrase Benjamin Franklin, "Early success has ruined many a good speaker."

It always bodes well for speakers—beginner or experienced—to immediately ask themselves when accepting an invitation, "To what do I attribute the success of my last speech?"

The honest answer will always be, "thorough preparation."

In Closing

I have three hopes.

First, I hope you have enjoyed reading this book about public speaking as much as I have enjoyed writing it. It has been a joy.

I also hope it has been informative.

Third, I hope that while you improve your speaking skills, you have a pleasant journey along the way.

Someone once asked Winston Churchill how to end a speech. He replied, "When you have said all you have to say and come to a sentence with a grammatical ending—sit down."

I think my time has come.

INDEX